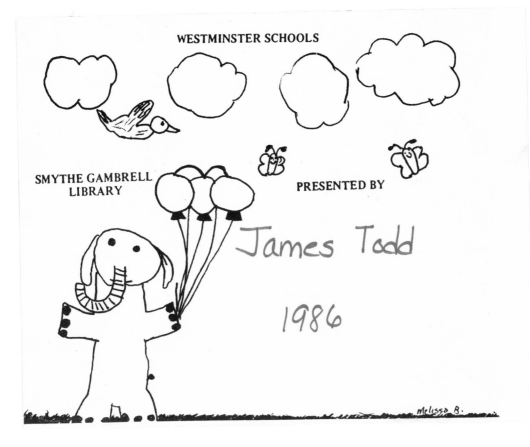

WESTMINSTER SCHOOLS

SMYTHE GAMBRELL
LIBRARY

PRESENTED BY

James Todd

1986

Melissa B.

PLANET EARTH

THE WORK OF THE WIND

David Lambert

The Bookwright Press
New York · 1984

PLANET EARTH

Coastlines
Volcanoes
The Oceans
Water on the Land
The Work of the Wind
Weather and Climate

First published in the United States in 1984 by
The Bookwright Press, 387 Park Avenue South,
New York, NY 10016

First published in 1983 by
Wayland (Publishers) Ltd
49 Lansdowne Place, Hove
East Sussex BN3 1HF, England

ISBN 0-531-04789-X

Library of Congress Catalog Card Number 83-72797

Printed in Italy by
G. Canale & C.S.p.A., Turin

Contents

Winds bring the rainy season to the Serengeti Plain in Africa.

4

What wind can do

Wind is nothing you can see or grasp—just moving air that you can feel. Something that hardly seems to be there at all might not seem to deserve having a book written about it. Yet if there were no wind, the world would be a very different place.

Without wind to take heat away from the world's hottest lands, the plants and animals there would die of overheating. Without wind to bring heat to the world's cooler countries, these would be forever frozen. Without wind to pick up moisture from the sea and shed it over land as rain, many areas would be too dry for plants and animals to live there. Without wind to carry their seeds, many plants would not have spread across the countryside.

However, some winds can have harsh effects on land and living things. Certain dry winds stop rain from reaching deserts, where few kinds of plants and animals can thrive. Wind even shapes the desert surface by slowly wearing the rocks away and heaping up their broken particles as piles of sand.

Cold or fierce winds can kill unprotected living things. But plants and animals that live in windy places have adapted in ways that help them to survive. People cope with harmful winds in other ways, with the inventions they have made. Man has even discovered how to put the energy in wind to work for him.

This book explains all these effects of winds, but first we shall see just how and why winds blow, and how they can be measured.

Wind-borne sand collects into great dunes.

Prevailing winds

These are steady winds, set in motion by the sun's heat driving air from hotter to cooler places on the Earth. Prevailing winds work like this: the sun strongly heats a broad belt of air above and near the **equator.** This heating makes the air thin out and expand, so it grows lighter than the cooler, denser air around it and floats up like hot air above a fire. This region of rising air forms a belt of calm air called the **doldrums.**

When the air has risen twice the height at which jet planes fly, it spreads out north and south from the equator. It cools as it spreads, growing heavier and sinking back to Earth. This happens about one-third of the way from the equator toward the North and South poles. The still regions of sinking air are known as the horse latitudes, because horses being carried across the Atlantic in sailing ships often used to die when the ships were stopped by the lack of wind. As the air sinks it is squashed, and as it warms up it presses strongly outward. Some of this

dense, high-pressure air flows low across the Earth back to the doldrums, filling the gap left by the rising, "thin" low-pressure air. It is rather like what happens when the high-pressure air in a tire rushes out from a puncture.

The warm air flowing from the horse latitudes toward the doldrums is called the **trade winds.** The name comes from the old phrase "to blow trade," which means to blow steadily in one direction.

The circulation of air above the equator.

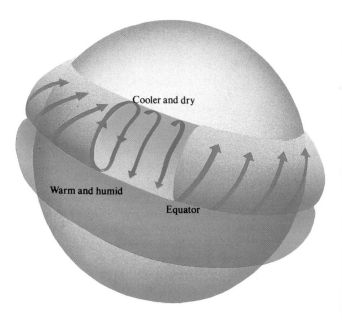

6

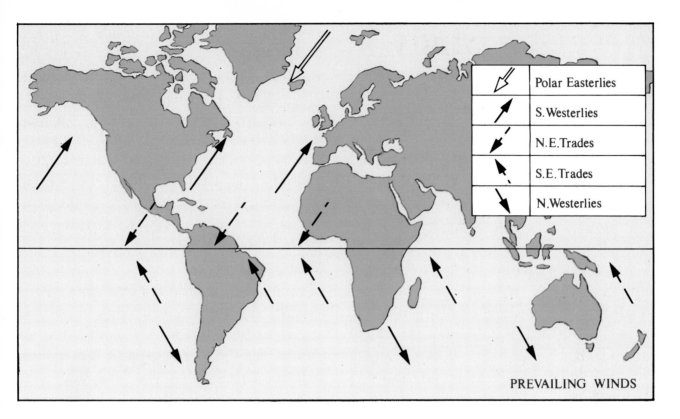

⬈	Polar Easterlies
↗	S. Westerlies
↙	N.E. Trades
↖	S.E. Trades
↘	N. Westerlies

PREVAILING WINDS

But some of the warm air from the horse latitudes blows toward the poles as so-called **westerlies.** About two-thirds of the way from the equator to the poles these westerlies meet the cold dense air of the **polar easterlies** blowing from the polar regions.

How winds are steered

Because the Earth is spinning, all these

These are the world's prevailing winds, which blow steadily in one direction all the year round.

prevailing winds cannot blow directly north or south. You can see why if you try to chalk a straight line down a turning globe. The line is curved. In the same way the Earth's spin steers winds to the right as they head north or south in the northern hemisphere, and to the left in the southern hemisphere. This is called the **Coriolis effect** after Gaspard Gustave de Coriolis, the French engineer who discovered it.

There are three belts of prevailing winds on each side of the equator, and the Earth's spin affects all of them. Westerlies try to head away from the equator but get steered from west to east. Trade winds and polar easterlies try to head toward the equator but are steered from east to west. Like many winds, these easterlies and westerlies are named after the direction from which they are blowing.

Winds of the upper atmosphere

In some regions winds blow around the world from west to east, high above the winds we have described. About 10 kilometers up (6 miles) great rivers of air writhe from side to side like snakes as they flow around the polar regions. Nearer the equator an airstream called the subtropical **jet stream** blows high above Africa, Asia and North America. Jet streams usually blow at 90 to 110 kilometers an hour (56 to 68 miles per hour), but at times they can reach speeds four times faster than this.

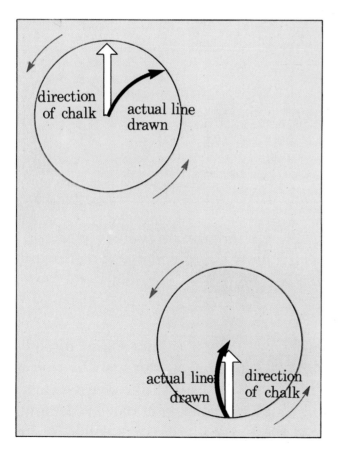

direction of chalk

actual line drawn

actual line drawn

direction of chalk

Left *The Coriolis effect demonstrated on a turntable.*

Wind speeds and weather forecasts

High winds have destroyed this wooden barn.

Sometimes the wind blows so slowly that you can scarcely feel it on your cheek. At other times it roars by like an express train. On the cold coast of Antarctica, winds reach 320 kilometers an hour (200 miles an hour). They have touched even higher speeds on Mt. Washington in the United States.

In 1805 a British admiral, Sir Francis Beaufort, invented a way to measure wind speed by its effects on sailing ships. Beaufort used numbers from 0 to 12 for winds of different strengths. Force Two, for instance, is a breeze strong enough for you to feel against your face. Force Six is a strong breeze that, on land, makes big branches sway and umbrellas difficult to use. Force Ten is a gale—a wind that uproots trees and may badly damage buildings. Force Twelve, **hurricane** force, causes terrible destruction.

Nowadays weather forecasters use instruments that measure wind speed exactly. One instrument is the cup-anemometer. This has several cups fixed to spokes jutting from a shaft. Wind pushes the cups, which in turn spin the shaft. The faster the wind blows, the faster the shaft turns. A special device measures its speed.

Weather vanes show wind direction. A weather vane has a flat blade that can turn east, west, north or south. When the wind blows on the blade, it lines up with the wind, and an electric meter or an arrow on a rod fastened to the blade shows the wind direction.

Meteorologists (scientists who study the weather) measure wind speed high in the air by releasing balloons filled with a light gas called helium. These weather balloons rise to a height of around 25,000 meters (76,000 feet), and drift with the wind. By tracking them with radar, scientists on the ground can measure the speed of the wind high above. With this information, weather experts draw special arrows on weather maps to show wind speed and direction. This helps them to forecast weather, because changes in wind speed and direction often mean changes in the weather.

Meteorologists releasing a weather balloon to measure wind speed.

Special winds

In any of the world's belts of prevailing winds, the wind may sometimes change and blow in any direction. This is because at times some of the air heats up or cools down more than the air around it.

Winds over land and sea

In many places, the wind that blows depends partly on how the land and sea affect the air above. Land warms up and cools down faster than water. This means that on a hot summer morning, the air above the land warms up quickly, thins out and rises. Meanwhile, the air above the sea is still cool, dense and heavy. So a cool sea breeze blows onshore to fill the gap left by the warm, rising air. At night, the opposite happens—the land cools down faster than the sea, and a land breeze blows offshore.

In a much bigger way, continents and oceans set winds blowing. For instance, in the freezing polar regions an air mass over the land is colder and denser, and so has

During the day, a cool breeze blows in from the sea.

At night, the breeze blows off the land.

higher pressure than the air mass over the nearby ocean. Winds try to flow out of the high-pressure air mass into the nearby low-pressure air mass. But because winds are steered by the Earth's spin, instead of traveling in a straight line, the winds actually blow around the center of each air mass. In the northern hemisphere winds blow counter-clockwise around each low-pressure air mass (a **cyclone**) and clockwise around each high-pressure air mass (an **anticyclone).** In the southern hemisphere, winds blow around the cyclones and anticyclones in the opposite directions.

As seasons change, these air masses and their winds may shift position. For example, winds called **monsoons** blow from the land to an ocean in winter, and from ocean onto the land in summer. Monsoons bring wet summers and dry winters to much of Asia. This is because winds passing over the oceans pick up moisture which falls on the land as rain, but winds blowing from inland are usually dry.

Cyclonic winds

Some air-pressure systems and their winds travel far around the world in only days. This happens at the polar fronts—the invisible shifting lines where the warm air

of the westerlies meets the cold air of the polar easterlies. Often, a tongue of warm air bulges out into the colder, denser polar air beyond a front.

But polar air cuts in from behind the tongue. Then a giant eddy of low-pressure air whirls eastward, bringing drizzle, cloud and showers. Such eddies as these form the cyclones also known as lows or **depressions.** They can measure up to 3,200 kilometers (2,000 miles) across. Every day depressions cross the northern and southern oceans. They die out only

Giant depressions wheel across the southern oceans.

when their warm air rises and the surrounding cold air flows in to fill the gap.

Low-pressure depressions with very low centers bring gales fierce enough to wreck ships and topple trucks. But tropical cyclones are even more intense and terrible. These storms are called *hurricanes* in the Gulf of Mexico and Caribbean Sea, *cyclones* in the Indian Ocean, *typhoons* in the China Seas, and *willy-willies* off northwest Australia. In a

The funnel of this tornado is dark because of the debris sucked up the vortex.

tropical cyclone, winds up to 270 kilometers an hour (170 miles an hour) range around a calm center called the "eye" of the hurricane.

The fiercest winds of all are those of a **tornado.** This looks like a writhing pillar of dust. The pillar moves no faster than a car. But inside, its winds whirl at up to 800 kilometers (500 miles) an hour. Air pressure in a tornado is so low that buildings in its path explode as the air inside them is sucked out. Hundreds of tornadoes happen every year in the United States' Mississippi Valley. Tornadoes form when warm, damp air from the Gulf of Mexico meets cold air from the north. At sea, such winds suck water high into the air as **waterspouts.**

Winds with special names

In some places depressions bring rather special local winds. Depressions that travel along the Mediterranean Sea pull warm winds north from Africa's hot, dry Sahara Desert. These winds have different names in different places. There is Egypt's *khamsin,* Italy's *sirocco,* Spain's *leveche,* and the *gibli,* which blows across Tunisia like a blast of hot air from an opened

oven. Similar hot winds include the *zonda* of Argentina and the *brickfielder*—a scorching wind in southeast Australia.

But depressions can bring cold winds from the polar regions too. Cold air pouring south down the valley of the Rhône River brings the fierce *mistral* wind to southern France. Texas has its chilly *norther.* Argentina suffers the cold *pampero,* and southeast Australia some-

A stifling dust storm blowing through a village in the Sudan.

times shivers under a *southerly-buster.* winter, strong polar winds pulled south by a depression bring storms of powdery snow called **blizzards** to North American prairies; and Siberia suffers from the dreaded *buran,* a fierce, cold, north and northeast wind.

Mountain winds

High mountain ranges have a dramatic effect on certain winds sucked in by depressions. The *chinook* is a famous mountain wind of Canada and the United States. It often blows east across the Rocky Mountains in spring and winter. The wind warms up as it descends from the mountains to the plains and quickly melts the lying snow. In fact "chinook" is an American Indian word that means "snow-eater." Similarly, the warm, dry *föhn* wind melts snow as it blows down the northern slopes of the European Alps.

At night, cold air sinks down the mountain, and fog develops in the valley.

By day, wind blows up the mountain.

Sometimes such winds set off the terrifying snow slides called avalanches.

Mountains do more than just affect winds blowing over them. They make winds of their own. By day, the sun's heat warms the air, which rises from the mountain slopes and valleys. To take its place, winds blow up the valleys. These winds are called **anabatic,** a name that comes from a Greek word meaning "to go up." By night the opposite happens. Cold, heavy air slides down the slopes and valleys. These are called **katabatic** winds, and blow particularly strongly from the ice caps covering the frozen mountains of Antarctica and Greenland.

An avalanche thunders down, close to a mountaineer's base camp.

Land attacked by wind

In places wind attacks and wears away the surface of the land. This happens mostly in the great dry areas called deserts. Winds even help to make and keep these desert regions dry.

How winds make deserts

Several factors can go to make a desert. The place may lie far inland, away from moist sea breezes bringing rain. It may always lie under dry, sinking air, so that

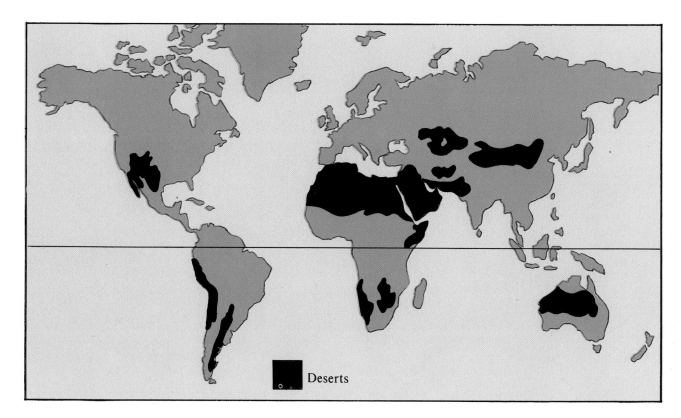

Deserts

dry winds blow outward and stop moist sea breezes from blowing in. Perhaps winds have come from the sea, but have shed their moisture on the way, either because they cooled as they climbed to cross a mountain range, or as they blew across a chilly ocean current.

Deserts lie in every continent except Antarctica and Europe. The deserts of Asia include Mongolia's Gobi Desert and the great Arabian Desert that covers most of Arabia. Most of northern Africa is taken up by the Sahara. Almost as big as the United States, this is the world's largest desert. Another big desert, the Kalahari, lies in southwest Africa. In North America, the Colorado Desert, Mojave Desert and others sprawl over much of the southwestern United States and Mexico. In South America, the narrow Atacama Desert lines much of the coast of Chile and Peru. Deserts also cover the center of Australia.

Desert winds at work

Some desert winds blow strongly and steadily for months. Others come and go. Many start because one patch of ground grows hotter than the land around it. The air above the heated patch thins out and rises. Then a **whirlwind** starts to blow around this small, low-pressure mass of air, lifting light particles of dust from the desert floor. Dusty whirlwinds a few feet across are called **dust devils.** They cross a desert like writhing pillars up to 1,000 meters (3,300 feet) high, but many of them soon die out. Large masses of

Left *A whirling dust devil snakes across the savannah.*

19

whirling, choking, dust-filled air are called **dust storms.**

If a wind blows fast enough to lift grains of sand high off the ground you have a **sandstorm.** Scorching sandstorms called *simooms* carry clouds of stinging sand raging over parts of the Sahara Desert.

Sand is the main weapon used by wind to rub away rocks rising from the desert

Below *Wind-sculpted sandstone in Nevada.*

surface. You may get some idea how this happens if you have felt windblown sand sting your ankles on a beach, or if you have seen anyone doing some sand-blasting, using a jet of air containing sand particles to clean and polish. Windblown sand attacks rocks up to the level of a man's waist; sand grains are too heavy for most winds to lift much higher than that. Small stones are even heavier, but strong winds send them hopping and skipping along the ground.

Rocks shaped by desert winds

Sometimes sand blows across a layer of rock that is all of the same hardness. The sand simply smooths and polishes the rock. Often, though, moving sand meets rocks made of soft and hard layers. Where a soft rock layer lies below a hard layer, sand rubs away the soft layer until the hard one stands perched on just a narrow stem of rock, and the whole shape looks like a giant mushroom.

If the hard and soft layers lie on their

Opposite *The wind has weathered these vertical layers of sandstone until they look like an elephant.*

sides, the wind sandblasts deep furrows in the soft layers but leaves the hard ones sticking up between them like strange walls or giant ribs of stone. In parts of Central Asia rows of rock ribs twice as tall as a man are separated by long corridors cut out by windborne sand. These rock formations are called *yardangs*. Wind-whipped sand can widen narrow cracks into a maze of gullies until the solid rock between the cracks shrinks into a strange forest of stone pillars.

In time, speeding sand helps to scour away any rock or stone standing in its path. It gouges shallow caves in the bottom of rocky hills and undercuts them until their sides become steep cliffs.

Sand rasps away at pebbles and gives them sharp-edged, streamlined shapes. Such pebbles are called **ventifacts,** which means "things shaped by wind." As sand grains rub on rock and one another, even they gradually wear away. Desert sand grains look like tiny, rounded millet seeds. They are smoother than sand grains shaped by seas or rivers. "Millet-seed" sand grains in some ancient sandstone rocks show that the rocks were formed, millions of years ago, from desert sands.

You can see such rocks in countries like England and Germany, which shows that long ago there were deserts in places where there are no deserts today. Careful study of scratch marks on the ancient sand grains in the rocks can show a scientist how fast the wind was blowing when it rubbed the grains against each other.

Rock basins

Desert winds do more than grind down hills and mountains until only level plains of solid rock remain. Winds attack the plains too.

This may happen if the hard rock surface cracks in a way that lets the wind-blown sand gnaw into the softer rock beneath. In time, sand may scrape out a hollow like a giant saucer. The world's largest wind-worn hollow is the Qattara Depression in Egypt. This dip is almost as big as the state of New Jersey, and its lowest part lies below sea level.

Shallower depressions of this kind lie in the deserts of Mongolia, southwest Africa, and western Australia. Many are deep enough to reach underground water that can be used for growing crops. Such fruitful places in a desert form **oases.**

In places, the desert may be worn away enough to reach underground water.

Desert trash heaps

While wind wears away rocks in one part of a desert, it must dump its load of broken fragments somewhere else. In this way wind builds huge heaps and sheets of sand and dust in the deserts and beyond.

Sands on the move

Desert winds heap up billions of sand grains to build level sheets of sand or low sand hills called **dunes.**

Dunes come in many shapes and sizes. Where the wind blows steadily from one direction, a heap of sand grains may lodge against a rock that blocks their path. Another heap collects behind the rock, sheltered from the wind. Such heaps are known as *head-and-tail dunes.* The head is short, but the tail—the heap of sand behind the rock—may measure from a few paces to 750 meters (nearly half a mile). Head-and-tail dunes cause eddies in the wind blowing by and slow it down. This helps more dunes to grow nearby.

Although many dunes collect around a stone or other obstacle, some seem to start on flat ground—no one knows just why. Among these types are the dunes called *barkhans.* A barkhan's low sides are blown forward faster than the high middle so they jut out like horns. As sand piles up against the gently sloping

Barkhans *and* seif *dunes in Namibia.*

windward side, the dune grows taller. Some barkhans are as high as a church steeple. As wind blows the sand across the top, the whole dune gradually creeps across the desert. Small barkhans may advance 15 meters (50 feet) a year. Swarms of barkhans advance across some parts of the Sahara Desert.

If wind direction changes, the barkhans may lose their horns and join up to make long rows of sharp-ridged dunes. Because they look a bit like wavy swords, these sandy hills are called *seif dunes. (Seif* is Arabic for "sword".)

Some of the seif dunes in Iran rise to 215 meters (700 feet), but Algeria has dunes twice as high as that. Wind blows strongly down the corridors between the seif dunes' ridges.

Instead of dunes, some hot deserts are covered by great sheets of sand. These sand seas tend to grow where a pebbly surface slows down the wind. This simply makes the wind drop its load of sand and the sand spreads out evenly among the pebbles.

Left *The flat plain of a pebbly desert.*

Sand dunes

Away from the deserts, winds heap up sands on many sandy shores. Strong winds blowing up a beach will drive sand inshore. Some of the sand lodges against a plant or lump of driftwood. So a sand dune starts to develop. In time rows of dunes lie side by side along the upper shore. Later their sides join up to make one long dune. If grass grows thickly on a dune, the grass roots and stems may hold the sand in place. As more sand piles up on top, the dune grows even higher. Southern Spain and western France have coastal dunes as tall as a skyscraper office block.

Sometimes walkers on the beach, or even rabbits, clear a sandy patch among the grasses on the seaward side of the belt of dunes. Then a "blow-out" happens. The wind blows the bare sand inland as a separate dune. This looks rather like a barkhan, but its curved ends trail back toward the sea. Where the old dune stood, new dunes grow and join together. The dip between the old and new dunes is called a slack. Sometimes row on row of dunes and slacks spread inland from a sandy beach.

Marram grass holds the sand in place on windswept dunes.

Windblown dust

Sands are too heavy to be carried very far by wind, but strong winds can whisk light particles of dust hundreds of miles. Dust from the Sahara Desert may settle on ships far out at sea. The red rain that sometimes falls on Britain is coloured by dust from the Sahara, more than a thousand miles away.

Winter winds blowing from the Gobi Desert have dumped huge quantities of dust on northern China. Here, an area of land bigger than France is covered by a layer of a crumbly, yellow substance, called **loess.** In places it lies 300 meters (1,000 feet) thick. Loess is so soft that carts and rivers quickly wear it away, until roads and rivers run through cuttings, between high loess cliffs. Many Chinese live in caves cut in the cliff walls.

Windblown dust also covers much of Europe, from France to Russia, as well as the midwest of the United States. People call this dust *limon* in France and *adobe* in America. But its particles are sharp edged, not rounded, like those of loess. Scientists think *limon* and *adobe* come not from deserts but rocks ground up by the heavy

Wind can carry desert dust high into the air.

27

ice sheets that once covered much of northern North America and Europe.

A road covered by snowdrifts after a blizzard.

Snow shaped by wind

Much as desert winds build dunes, so strong wintry winds pile snow into snow-drifts. Snowdrifts grow where fences, walls and hedges obstruct the wind, and in sheltered spots where wind sheds its snowy load.

In polar regions, steady winds pile snow into long ridges called **sastrugi.** Sastrugi look rather like the seif dunes of a desert. If an explorer knows which way the pre-vailing wind blows, he can use sastrugi as pointers to guide him across a snowfield.

Wind, plants, and animals

The wind can be both enemy and friend to plants and animals. Some living things have special ways of defending themselves against injury from the wind and many make the wind work for them.

Wind as an enemy

Wind can injure living things by its sheer strength. Fierce winds can damage vegetation. The winter gales that sweep across mountains snap branches off trees and rip up chunks of turf. On sandy shores dunes may be blown away, scattering the plants that grow upon them.

Similarly, wind can damage animals. Strong winds blow away countless tiny insects. Hurricanes and tornadoes can pick up larger creatures too. Earthworms, salamanders, kangaroo-rats and even a tortoise have been carried through the air. When the wind slows down, the creatures drop to the earth. People have seen tiny frogs falling in a shower of rain. Even fish sucked up by a waterspout may fall gasping on dry land. Millions of small land

These trees in Sri Lanka were damaged by a typhoon.

creatures are blown into the sea and drowned.

Lastly, cold winds can injure living things by chilling and drying. Unprotected animals may freeze to death in winter gales. Plants suffer more damage from drying out. This is because wind pulls moisture from their leaves. The leaves get their moisture from the plants' roots,

Beech trees shaped by cold prevailing winds.

which suck water from the soil. But the roots cannot suck up water if the soil is frozen. When this happens, leaves exposed to wind dry out and die. This occurs especially on windy cliffs, cold mountain tops and in the cold far north and far south. On sea cliffs, cold prevailing winds will kill the leaves on the windward side of each tree trunk, and bend its growing twigs so that branches stream out from the sheltered side like flags. On cold mountain tops and in chilly Arctic lands, winter winds may kill off any shoots that peep above the winter snow. Here, the trees may grow only knee-high.

Resisting the wind

Plants and animals that are used to living in windy places can survive the fiercest gales. Grass stems, and the trunks and branches of some trees, bend before the wind instead of breaking. Other trees may have branches too strong and tough to be snapped off by storms. Trees growing on cliff ledges grip soil and rock with roots like claws.

Some species of small flowering plants hug the ground like rounded cushions. Their smooth shapes protect the plants from the worst the wind can do.

Trees such as oaks and maples are not dried up by winter winds because they shed their leaves in winter. Firs and spruces keep their leaves in winter, but these tough, narrow "needles" do not lose moisture easily.

Animals survive harsh winds in other ways. When strong winds blow, mosquitoes hide among the undergrowth. Otherwise these light flying insects would

Left *This small* roseroot *plant grows close to the rock and escapes wind damage.*

be whisked away. Some insects on windy, remote islands of the southern oceans are even safer, because they never fly. For example, eighteen out of twenty kinds of insects that live on Tristan da Cunha have tiny wings or none at all. One is a fly with tiny shrunken wings; another is a wingless moth.

Small mammals such as shrews and field mice avoid cold winds by hiding in burrows. Bigger mammals such as mountain sheep and goats dig hollows in the snow to shelter from winter gales. Such beasts also grow chill-proof coats. The strongest winds cannot penetrate a yak's thick, matted wool, the dense fur of a mountain leopard, or the downy feathers of an emperor penguin.

Thick feathers protect these penguins.

This strange fungus has just released a cloud of spores.

How plants use wind

Various plants use wind in one way or another. The lightest breeze carries millions of tiny pollen grains shed by flowering plants such as grasses and oak trees. Pollen grains that land on female flowers produce seeds from which new plants can grow.

Wind can also help to spread plant seeds themselves. Orchid seeds no bigger than a speck of dust may float hundreds

Tumbleweed blows across the prairie.

of miles in the air. So may the spores of mosses, ferns and fungi. Spores are so tiny that 400 laid side by side would make a row less than half an inch long. Winds carry billions of tiny seeds and spores far and wide. Some have landed and sprouted on islands newly risen from the sea. No wonder that the first plants growing on new land are often mosses, ferns and fungi.

Some larger, heavier seeds are shaped in ways that help them travel with the wind. Dandelion and thistle seeds hang from stalks with tiny hairy parachutes. Seeds of pines and sycamores have wings; they drift down from their parent trees, spinning like little helicopters.

North America's tumbleweed plants spread in a different way. When they have died, the wind snaps off the plants and rolls them far across the prairies, where they scatter their seeds as they go.

How animals use wind

At any moment on a summer's day millions of tiny living things are drifting on the breeze that blows above your head. Many of these travelers are animals. Some small creatures hitch a ride upon the wind to find new homes. Tiny spiders climb plants and shoot silken threads into the wind. The wind whisks threads and spiders far away before they float gently to earth again. In this way spiders and small caterpillars travel from one mountain to the next. High up on the tallest peaks in the world, tiny mites and insects eat seeds and dead insects wafted up by the wind from far below.

Bigger insects such as desert locusts also ride the wind. First, winds whirl locusts into the center of a depression. Here, rain falls on the dry land and plants grow quickly. Thousands of locusts land, eat the plants, and lay their eggs. Huge numbers hatch. When the young grow wings, they also travel with the wind. A locust swarm weighing a thousand tons or more may fly far over North Africa and cross the Red Sea.

Gliding and soaring birds make use of

The wind can carry locusts aloft in thousands.

moving air. Albatrosses have very long wings, and they glide around the southern oceans on the strong westerlies which blow around Antarctica. Eagles, with broader wings, soar high on rising currents of warm air.

Vultures gliding on motionless wings.

Migrating birds use winds to help them reach summer breeding grounds or winter homes. Redwings, a species of thrush, use the winds blowing around a depression to speed them south from Iceland to Spain.

Surprising things can happen when winds blow birds off course. In the early 1900s, trade winds blew a flock of cattle egrets from Africa to South America. These white herons settled there and bred. Now they have even reached the United States. In the same way, wind-blown land birds long ago reached the Hawaiian Islands far out in the Pacific Ocean.

Every year stray birds and even some butterflies are blown across the broad Atlantic Ocean all the way from North America to Europe.

Wind and man

Wind affects our lives in more ways than you might suppose. Also, some of our most useful discoveries and inventions have been those that prevent or overcome the damage done by wind, and those that make the wind do useful work.

Hot and cold wind

Winds can both help and harm the human body. This is because air blowing past your skin takes away some body heat. Losing heat may make you feel pleasantly cooler if you had been overheated by hot, still, damp air. On the other hand, the people used to living on the steamy, tropical coast of West Africa do not look forward to the wind called the *harmattan*. This very dry and dusty wind blows in from the Sahara every winter. It not only dries out their skin, but it can spoil their crops as well.

In cold, frosty weather, wind may have a very different effect. Still, cold air can feel quite pleasant. But even a light breeze may make you feel uncomfortably cold.

Wind-whipped snow can feel bitterly cold.

This **windchill** effect is worst where cold storm winds cross polar lands and high mountains. Bitterly cold winds can kill the skin of unprotected noses, ears, toes and fingers. This causes frostbite. Many explorers, travelers and mountaineers caught in blizzards have died from the terrible effects of windchill.

When storms rage

Most wind damage comes from the sheer force of a mass of fast-moving air. Hurricane-strength winds have blown down many unsafe buildings. One stormy night in 1879 Scotland's Tay Bridge fell into the river below and took a train down with it. In 1940 a fairly mild gale destroyed the new Tacoma Narrows Bridge in the state of Washington. First its roadway rippled up and down, then a large chunk in the middle broke away and fell.

Even stronger winds inflict worse damage. In 1925 a tornado killed nearly 700 people in the southern United States. In 1963 Hurricane Flora crossed the Caribbean Sea; more than 6,000 people died and three-quarters of a million homes were blown down.

Strong winds are also damaging because of what they blow away. In 1934 millions of tons of precious topsoil just whirled away from farms in Kansas, Texas, and Oklahoma. The real reason was bad farming. Farmers had overused the soil so that it lacked plant roots strong or deep enough to hold soil particles together. Windblown dust and sand can be a nuisance where they settle. Creeping sand dunes may engulf oases in a desert or invade the farms around its edge.

Sometimes winds bring other harmful things. Flames and sparks borne by the wind spread forest fires. Chemicals in the smoke from some factory chimneys are carried up into the air, and fall back to earth far away as acid in the rain. This acid rain is slowly killing thousands of trees in the forests of Scandinavia and Germany.

Opposite *Oklahoma in the 1930s. The farmers ploughed up the fertile grassland to plant crops. With no grass roots to hold the soil, high winds and drought created a man-made desert called a dust bowl.*

SD-5089

Coping with the wind

Luckily there are ways to cope with many of these problems. Windproof clothes and shelters protect most of us from the effects of windchill. Tall hedges or rows of such trees as cypresses protect orchards from wind damage. In Libya, Egypt and Israel farmers plant belts of acacia and eucalyptus to keep desert sands from drifting over fields. In Iran, oil is spread on sand to keep the wind from blowing sand from around the roots of newly planted tamarisks. Along sandy shores, planting marram grass on dunes helps prevent them from invading nearby land.

Scientific know-how enables engineers to build bridges that can withstand the worst storms. Also, farmers who keep their soil well nourished prevent the wind from blowing it away. To stop fires from spreading, foresters cut broad tracks through a forest. Unless the wind blows very hard indeed it cannot carry flames and sparks across these firebreaks. To keep poisonous chemicals out of smoke,

Right *Planting trees stops desert dunes from drifting.*

40

Sailing ships use the power of the wind to cross the world's oceans.

some factories clean the smoke before it leaves their chimneys. But not all factories can afford this costly cleaning, so acid rain may go on killing forests.

Machines that use the wind

People have long been building machines that use the energy in wind to help them move about. Over four thousand years ago, the Egyptians invented sailing ships with square sails. They only worked well when the wind pushed from behind, but by the 1500s explorers sailed the world in better vessels. Square sails were hung across the ship, and a three-sided sail pointed forward and back. This lateen sail helped a ship to make better headway

41

Left *Hot air balloons can be carried over great distances by the wind.*

against the wind.

Big modern ships are mostly powered by oil, but oil is growing scarcer, so engineers have begun to design new kinds of sailing ships to carry large cargoes.

Meanwhile, thousands of people sail small yachts for fun or sport. There are even boats on wheels that sail across the sand, and iceboats that glide along on runners. Some iceboats can whizz over frozen lakes and rivers faster than 200 kilometers an hour (125 miles an hour).

Wind also helps man travel through the air in gliders or beneath balloons. Gliders use warm, rising air currents and the winds that blow up hills. These help the gliders soar and stay aloft. In 1978 winds blew a balloon carrying three people all the way across the Atlantic Ocean from the United States to France. Even airline pilots get help from the wind. They hitch a ride upon the very high jet streams that blow around the world from west to east.

While some inventors found how to use wind to help man travel, others harnessed wind for other useful jobs. Thirteen hundred years ago windmills were invented in Iran. The sails of the windmills turned wheels and axles that raised water from rivers to thirsty fields. Later came windmills to grind wheat into flour.

Today, engineers are building huge windmills called **aerogenerators,** to produce electric current. In a fresh gale, one of the biggest of these aerogenerators could generate enough power to provide electric lighting for a small town. One day, perhaps, forests of aerogenerators on hilltops or standing in the sea will supply windy lands with a large part of their electricity supply.

For centuries, windmills have used the power of the wind to grind wheat into flour.

Facts and figures

The Beaufort Scale. This scale of numbers shows wind speeds. The first Beaufort Scale went from Force 0 to Force 12. In 1955, the United States Weather Bureau added Forces 13 to 17.

Force	miles per hour	Type of wind
0	0-1	Calm
1	1-3	Light air
2	4-7	Light breeze
3	8-12	Gentle breeze
4	13-18	Moderate breeze
5	19-24	Fresh breeze
6	25-31	Strong breeze
7	32-38	High wind
8	39-46	Fresh gale
9	47-54	Strong gale
10	55-63	Whole gale
11	64-75	Storm
12	76-82	Hurricane
13	83-92	Hurricane
14	93-103	Hurricane
15	104-114	Hurricane
16	115-125	Hurricane
17	126-136	Hurricane

The highest recorded surface wind speed is 231 miles per hour at Mt. Washington, USA.

The windiest place on Earth is George V Coast, Antarctica, which has gales of up to 200 miles per hour.

The highest wind speed recorded in a tornado is 280 miles per hour.

An average tornado measures a quarter of a mile (400 meters) across.

A hurricane can measure from 50 to 250 miles across.

A depression can vary in size from 90 miles across to as much as 2,000 miles.

There are on average between 500 and 600 tornadoes per year in the United States, and the North American coasts are hit each year by an average of 11 hurricanes.

Deserts are the areas of the Earth most affected by the work of the wind: the largest is the Sahara Desert (3.25 million square miles), followed by the Australian Desert (600,000 square miles), the Arabian Desert (500,000 square miles), and the Gobi Desert (400,000 square miles).

Approximately one-third of the Earth's land surface is desert, or extremely dry.

Each year the deserts of the world spread by 20,000 square miles, and there are 14.5 million square miles of land at risk of turning into desert.

Glossary

Aerogenerator A huge two-bladed windmill that uses the power of the wind to turn a turbine to generate electricity.

Anabatic wind A local wind that blows by day up a mountain slope or mountain valley.

Anticyclone A large mass of dense, high-pressure air. Winds blow clockwise around anticyclones in the northern hemisphere and counterclockwise in the southern hemisphere.

Blizzard A storm in which strong winds whip up snow until you cannot see through it.

Coriolis effect The tendency of the Earth's spin to bend winds and ocean currents to their right in the northern hemisphere and to their left in the southern hemisphere.

Cyclone A mass of low-pressure air with unsettled weather. Winds blow counterclockwise around cyclones in the northern hemisphere, and clockwise in the southern.

Depression A cyclone bringing windy, cloudy, rainy weather in cool parts of the world.

Doldrums A windless belt at the equator, where warm air rises.

Dune A mound of sand heaped up by winds blowing across a desert, or up a sandy shore.

Dust devils Narrow, writhing, desert whirlwinds, full of dust. They are only a few meters across but can reach over 1,000 meters (3,300 feet) in height.

Equator An imaginary line making a circle around the Earth, halfway between the North and South Poles.

Hurricane A tropical cyclone with fierce winds. Any wind of Force 12 or above on the Beaufort Scale is also called a hurricane.

Jet stream A powerful wind blowing from west to east high above the ground. Several jet streams circle the Earth.

Katabatic wind A local wind caused by cold heavy air flowing down a mountain slope or valley, usually at night.

Loess Fine dust that is blown from desert areas by prevailing winds, and settles in other areas as a crumbly layer of soil.

Monsoon A wind system in which prevailing winds reverse direction from season to season.

Oases Places in a desert where water reaches the surface of the land, and vegetation can grow.

Polar easterlies Prevailing winds bringing cold air from the polar regions. They blow from the northeast in the northern hemisphere, and from the southeast in the southern hemisphere.

Prevailing winds Winds which blow steadily in one direction.

Sandstorm A storm in which strong winds blow a mass of sand grains above the ground. (Dust storms lift only particles of dust).

Sastrugi Snow ridges heaped up by the wind.

Tornado A small, very violent whirlwind,

common in the south central United States.

Trade winds Prevailing tropical winds blowing from northeast to southwest in the northern hemisphere, and from southeast to northwest in the southern hemisphere.

Ventifact A pebble or stone shaped by wind-blown sand.

Waterspout A column of water that is sucked up from the sea by a tornado. Waterspouts reach a height of 300 meters (1,000 feet).

Westerlies Prevailing winds between the Polar easterlies and trade winds. They blow from the southwest in the northern hemisphere, and from the northwest in the southern hemisphere.

Whirlwind A small pillar of air spinning around a low pressure center.

Windchill effect What happens when a cold wind chills your body by removing body heat.

Further reading

Alth, Max and Charlotte. *Disastrous Hurricanes and Tornadoes.* New York: Franklin Watts, 1981.

Broekel, Ray. *Storms.* Chicago: Childrens Press, 1982.

Caudil, Rebecca. *Wind, Sand and Sky.* New York: Dutton, 1976.

Fradin, Dennis. *Hurricanes, Disaster!.* Chicago: Childrens Press, 1982.

Fradin, Dennis. *Tornadoes.* Chicago: Childrens Press, 1982.

Lambert, David. *Weather.* New York: Franklin Watts, 1983.

Lampton, Christopher. *Meteorology: An Introduction.* New York: Franklin Watts, 1981.

Marko, Katherine D. *How the Wind Blows.* Nashville, Tennessee: Abingdon Press, 1981.

Payne, Sherry. *Wind and Water Energy.* Milwaukee, Wisconsin: Raintree Publishers, 1982.

Santrey, Lawrence. *What Makes the Wind.* Mahwah, N.J.: Troll Associates, 1981.

Smith, Norman. *Wind Power.* New York: Coward, McCann and Geoghegan, 1981.

Index

Picture acknowledgements

The illustrations in this book came from the following sources: from the Alan Hutchison Library—Alan Hutchison 15, 27, 41, A. Jennings 42, J. L. Peyromaure 29; Heather Angel 20, 21, 31, 33, 34; from Aquila Photographics—R. Gill 32, D. K. Richards 36; Anthony Bannister/N.H.P.A. 35; N. M. Browne 23; from Bruce Coleman Limited—Chris Bonnington 17, W. Carlson/Lane 14, Robert Carr 9, Geoff Dore 28, Jennifer Fry 5, Carol Hughes 24, J. Pearson 4, G. D. Plage 25, Hans Reinhard 30, R. Tidman 43, WWF/H. Jungius 26; Crown Copyright reserved 10, 13; Peter Newark's Western Americana 39; Malcolm S. Walker 6, 7, 8, 11, 12, 16, 18; Wayland Picture Library 40; Zefa 19, 37.